What Can You Do with a

PAPER BAG?

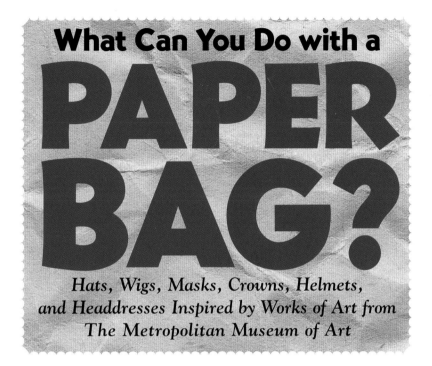

What Can You Do with a
PAPER BAG?

Hats, Wigs, Masks, Crowns, Helmets,
and Headdresses Inspired by Works of Art from
The Metropolitan Museum of Art

by Judith Cressy

Photography of children by Maria Quiroga and Christine A. Butler
Illustrations by Edward Heins

chronicle books · san francisco

in association with

THE METROPOLITAN MUSEUM OF ART

The works of art in this book are from the collections of The Metropolitan Museum of Art.

First Edition
Printed in Hong Kong

Produced by the Department of Special Publications, The Metropolitan Museum of Art: Robie Rogge, Publishing Manager; Judith Cressy, Project Editor; Anna Raff, Designer; Jennifer Van Dalsen, Production Associate.

Photography of works of art by The Metropolitan Museum of Art Photograph Studio unless otherwise noted.

Library of Congress Cataloging-in-Publication Data

Cressy, Judith.

What can you do with a paper bag? : hats, wigs, masks, crowns, helmets and headdresses inspired by works of art from the Metropolitan Museum of Art/by Judith Cressy ; photographs by Maria Quiroga and Christine Butler ; illustrations by Edward Heins.

    p. cm.
    ISBN 0-8118-3220-1
    1. Paper work-Juvenile literature. 2. Paper bags-Juvenile literature.
[1. Paper work. 2. Paper bags. 3. Handicraft.] I. Quiroga, Maria, ill. II. Butler, Christine, ill. III. Heins, Edward, ill. IV. Metropolitan Museum of Art (New York, N.Y.) V. Title.
TT870.C75 2001
745.54—dc21
    00-013162

ISBN 0-87099-975-3 (MMA)
ISBN 0-8118-3220-1 (Chronicle Books)

Distributed in Canada by Raincoast Books
9050 Shaughnessy Street, Vancouver, British Columbia V6P 6E5

10 9 8 7 6 5 4 3 2 1

Chronicle Books LLC
85 Second Street
San Francisco, California 94105

Visit the Museum's Web site: www.metmuseum.org
Visit the Chronicle Books Web site: www.chroniclebooks.com/Kids

Contents

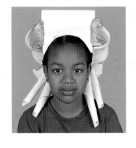

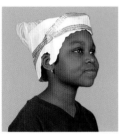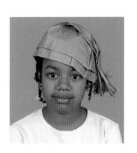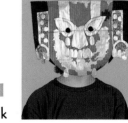

WHAT CAN YOU DO WITH A PAPER BAG?

As you are about to discover, the answer is "plenty!"

The twenty-one hats, wigs, and masks in this book all began with an ordinary paper bag and a little imagination. We got our inspiration by looking at everything from ancient Egyptian sculpture to twentieth-century fashion in the galleries of The Metropolitan Museum of Art. When you've tried making a few of these projects, take a look around your own environment. Use our techniques to make hats, wigs, and masks inspired by things you find on the pages of books or magazines, in store windows, or in the movies.

The children who modeled our paper-bag creations deserve special mention. Mikah Butler, Natalia Charles, Nicolas Conard, Gracianna Coscia, Raven Henderson, Georgina Renée Johnson, Lorant Lee, Bree Livingston, Jade Livingston, Tobias Levy, Karina Ruth Caballero-Patterson, William Salwen, Olivia Simone Sandiford, and Lily Susman appear on the cover of the book and throughout its pages.

MAKING THE PROJECTS

Skill levels: Each project is labeled "easy," "intermediate," or "advanced." Young children may need adult supervision at all skill levels, particularly in handling scissors. The initial steps for most of the projects include measuring, drawing lines, and folding, which may require adult help. The techniques for decorating the hats, wigs, and masks are simple, and children of all ages will be able to participate.

Introduction

Materials and techniques: Every project in this book can be made with common craft supplies. You'll need a ruler, a pencil, scissors, white glue, or transparent tape for almost all of the projects. Others also require construction or scrap paper, acrylic or poster paint, glitter glue, ribbon, string, pom-poms, and buttons. Be creative: If you don't have pom-poms, use stickers or paper cutouts, or simply paint the decoration instead.

Choosing a bag: Our bags come from local supermarkets and delis, and two are gift bags left over from last year's winter holidays. The instructions for each project include the dimensions of the grocery or gift bag required. Deli bags and other paper bags are usually stamped with a number indicating their size. Size 12 and size 16 bags are used throughout this book. A size 12 bag will fit most children's heads. Many teenagers and adults will need a size 16. Very small children might be able to wear a size 10. Be sure to try the bag on your head to make sure it fits before beginning a project.

If the bags you find are not labeled with their sizes, the following measurements correspond:
size 12 bag—7 x 13½ x 4⅜ inches
size 16 bag—7⅝ x 15½ x 4⅞ inches

BASIC INSTRUCTIONS

These techniques are used in projects throughout this book.

Rolling tape: Your finished hats and wigs will look much nicer if the tape used in making them is hidden. That is easily done by using small rolls of tape to attach pieces of paper. Cut a piece of tape 1 to 1½ inches long. Roll the tape, sticky side out, and overlap the ends slightly, as shown at right. Insert the rolls between two pieces of paper.

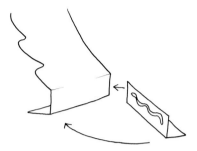 

2 *Attaching hinges*: To make wings stand out at right angles to a hat, attach them with hinges. Make a ¾-inch-deep fold at the end of the wing that will be attached to the hat. Measure the length of the fold. Draw a rectangle the length of the fold and 1½ inches wide on a piece of construction paper or other sturdy craft paper. Cut out the rectangle and fold it in half lengthwise. Put a line of glue on one side of the folded rectangle and attach it to the wing, as shown above. When the glue has dried, the wing can be glued or taped to the hat.

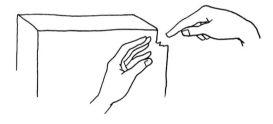

3 *Tucking-in corners*: Finished projects will look more like hats and less like paper bags if you tuck in the corners. To do so, place one hand inside the bag, with your fingers supporting a corner. Use the index finger of your other hand to poke in the corner as shown above right. Pinch and flatten the poked corner inside the bag. Secure it inside with a piece of tape, if desired. After a couple of tries, you will be able to make rounded corners or diagonal corners, depending on the look you want to achieve.

Blue-Ribbon Bonnet

EASY

size 12 or 16 paper bag

pencil

ruler

scissors

8½" x 11" sheet of construction paper or other mediumweight craft paper

transparent tape

5 feet of ribbon

Women's fashions in the 1830s and 1840s were very romantic. Full skirts and bonnets that framed the face and shaded the skin were in vogue.

Straw Bonnet
American, 1845–49
Natural leghorn straw
Gift of Edgar J. Lorie, Inc., in memory of
Laddie Northridge, 1960   CI60.23.36
Photograph by Sheldan Collins

1 Open the bag. Cut down the center of one of the narrow sides of the bag to about 4 inches from the bottom. Turning the scissors, cut to the fold on both sides of the center, as shown at right.

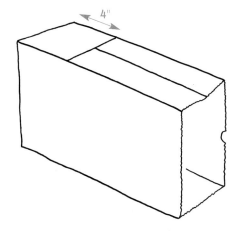

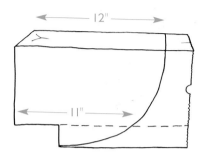

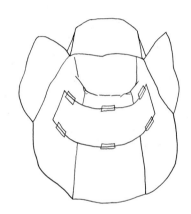

2 Open the two flaps out, and turn the bag flap-side down. Flatten the bag slightly at the open end, lining up the edges. Draw an arch shape on the bag, as shown at left. Then cut along the line, cutting through both layers of the bag at once, to create a 12-inch bonnet.

3 Open the bonnet. To give the back of the bonnet a rounded shape, tuck in all four corners, as shown in the Basic Instructions on page 11.

4 To give the top of the bonnet a rounded shape, fold the piece of construction paper in half lengthwise. Tape it inside the bonnet about 2 inches from the back, as shown at left.

5 Turn the bonnet right-side up. Cut a slit, just wide enough for the ribbon to pass though, in the fold of each side flap as shown at left. Gently ease the ribbon through each slit. Fold the flaps up slightly.

God of Wealth's Hat

EASY

- size 12 paper bag
- pencil
- ruler
- scissors
- 2 sheets of construction paper or other mediumweight to heavyweight craft paper
- glitter glue
- 2 buttons
- white glue
- transparent tape

The god of wealth was a very popular deity in China. Shown here seated on a gilded silver throne, he wears his most sumptuous clothing, including a filigreed hat with pearls, jade, and kingfisher feathers.

The God of Wealth in Military Aspect
Chinese, late 17th or early 18th century
Porcelain painted in polychrome overglaze enamels, pearls, jade, and kingfisher feathers, H. 22⅝ in.
Bequest of John D. Rockefeller Jr., 1960   61.200.12 a-c
Photograph by Schecter Lee

1 Starting with the bag folded flat, cut the bag crosswise so that it measures 5 inches from the bottom. Discard the cutoff piece.

2 Crease the bottom of the bag across the center so that it indents slightly, as shown at right. Open the bag and turn it bottom-side up.

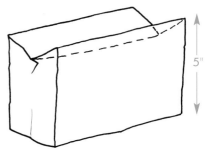

5"

3 Using the templates on pages 58 and 59, draw the outlines of the side piece, the front band, and the top crest on the construction paper, making two side pieces. Cut the shapes out of the construction paper.

4 Use the glitter glue to decorate the cutout pieces and the front of the hat following our designs, or any way you like. Make sure that the side pieces are facing in opposite directions when you decorate them.

5 While the glitter glue is drying, make and attach the hinges for the side pieces, as shown in the Basic Instructions, page 11.

6 When the glitter glue has dried, glue the buttons to the center front of the hat and the center of the front band for "jewels."

7 Attach the side pieces, the front band, and the top crest to the bag with white glue or rolls of tape. The hinges on the side panels should line up with the lower edge of the bag so that the panels slope downward toward the shoulders.

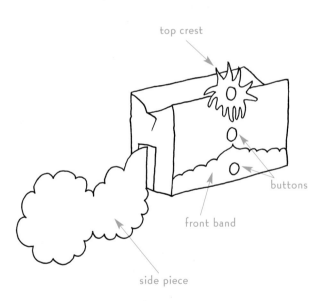

top crest

buttons

front band

side piece

Flower-Decorated Cloche

INTERMEDIATE

size 16 paper bag

pencil

ruler

scissors

drawing paper

acrylic paint
[blue, white, red, yellow, green]

paintbrush

colored pencils

white glue

Cloche
French, 1920s
Brown silk crepe and
polychrome silk ribbon
Label: Nicole Groult, 29 rue d'Anjou
Gift of Louise Morgan Hook, John P.
Morgan II and Anne Morgan
Simoneau, in memory of Mrs. Junius
S. Morgan, 1975   1975.296.1

*Fashioned in the 1920s, this hat sports
a bouquet of flowers cleverly made
from bits of silk ribbon and rickrack, all
with embroidered centers. Make the
flowers for your hat with painted paper.*

1 Starting with the bag folded flat, cut the bag crosswise 9 inches from the bottom. Discard the cutoff piece. Open the bag.

2 Fold the open end of the bag to the inside, to a depth of 4 inches. Set the bag bottom-side up.

3 To create the brim of the hat, choose one of the narrow sides of the bag to be the front of the hat. Use both hands to turn up the front edge of the bag to a depth of 1¼ inches. Slope the brim gradually toward the back of the hat, as shown at right. The back of the hat has no brim.

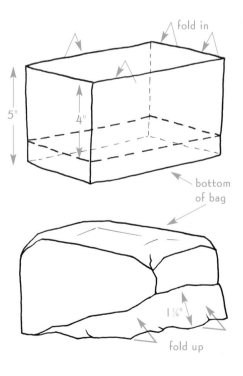

fold in

5"

4"

bottom
of bag

1¼"

fold up

4 To round the top of the hat, tuck in the four corners, as shown in the Basic Instructions, page 11.

5 Outline and paint a variety of flowers, leaves, and stems on drawing paper, creating them from your imagination or from the templates on page 59. Make seven flowers, seven leaves, and six stems. When the paint has dried, use the colored pencils to add details to the flowers and leaves.

6 Cut out the flowers, leaves, and stems, and glue them in place on the right side of the hat. Start by gluing the stems in place, angling them down toward the back of the hat. Glue the flowers and leaves on top of the stems.

Mayan Lord's Hat

EASY

size 12 paper bag

pencil

scissors

3 sheets of construction paper or other mediumweight to heavyweight craft paper

blue colored pencil or crayon

white glue

transparent tape

stickers, buttons, or pom-poms

More than a thousand years ago, Mayan lords in Mexico wore feathered costumes on important occasions. This man is thought to be a ruler because he is fat and richly dressed. His tall, branchlike hat, which is very unusual, has feathers at each side.

Mayan Costumed Figure
Mexico, 8th century
Ceramic, H. 11½ in.
The Michael C. Rockefeller Memorial Collection,
Gift of Nelson A. Rockefeller, 1970   1970.206.953

1 Start by making the "feathered" front and side pieces of the hat. Using the templates on pages 62 and 63, draw the outlines of the pieces on the construction paper. Make one front piece and two side pieces. Cut the shapes out of the construction paper.

2 Using the colored pencil or crayon, color the front and side pieces lightly, to give them a feathery look. Make sure that the side pieces are facing in opposite directions when you color them.

3 Make the hinges for attaching the side pieces to the hat. Directions for hinges are shown in the Basic Instructions on page 11.

4 Open the bag and place it bottom-side up, using one of the narrow sides of the bag as the front of the hat.

5 Use glue or small rolls of tape to attach the front and side pieces to the bag, placing the side pieces as close to the front as possible. The bottom of the hinges on the side pieces should line up with the open edge of the bag, as shown at right.

6 Decorate the front of the hat by attaching three rows of the stickers, buttons, or pom-poms. You can also use the paint to decorate the front of the hat.

Ribboned Cap

INTERMEDIATE

size 12 paper bag

pencil

ruler

scissors

white glue

2 yards of ribbon

transparent tape

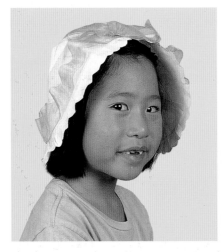

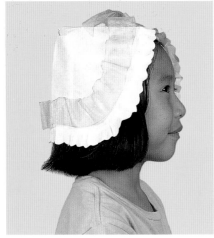

When indoors, 18th-century ladies of fashion topped their hairdos with ruffled silk caps, bound with satin ribbons.

The Love Letter (detail)
Jean Honoré Fragonard, French, 1732–1806
Oil on canvas, 32¼ x 26⅜ in.
The Jules Bache Collection, 1949   49.7.49

1 Start with the bag folded flat and the bottom of the bag facing upward. Draw the cutting line on the bag as shown in the diagram at right. Cut along the line, cutting through all the layers of the bag. Reserve the cutoff piece. Cut a "V" into the top front, as shown at right.

2 Open the cap out, as shown at right. To give the top of the cap a rounder look, tuck in the back corners, as shown in the Basic Instructions, page 11.

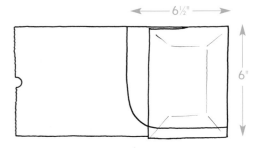

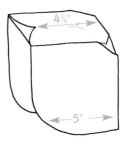

3 Using the reserved piece of bag, cut three strips, each about 1 inch wide and 13 inches long. Cut a scalloped edge along one edge of each strip. Then fold each strip into ¼-inch accordion folds, as shown at right.

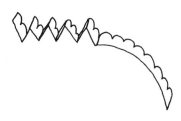

4 Open the strips out again so that they have a slightly ruffled surface. Starting at the top center of the cap, put a thin line of glue along the outside edge of the cap for 3 or 4 inches.

5 Pick up one of the strips, scalloped side out, and glue it along the edge of the cap. Continue this way, 3 to 4 inches at a time, all the way around the edge of the cap. Where it is necessary to ease the strip around curves, simply press small folds into the strip. Allow the glue to dry.

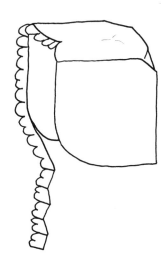

6 Starting at the top center, use small dots of glue or rolls of tape to attach the ribbon to the cap at intervals. Arrange the ribbon loosely so that it has a ruffled look. When you arrive back at the top of the cap, cut off the remaining ribbon, tie it into a bow, and glue the bow in place.

Fang Mask

EASY

small grocery bag [10¼" x 14¼" x 6⅛"]

10" dinner plate

pencil

ruler

scissors

acrylic paint [black, white]

paintbrush

cup of water for rinsing the paintbrush

black felt-tip pen

white glue

Janus-Faced Helmet Mask
Gabon, Fang people, 19th–20th century
Wood, paint, H. 11¾ in.
The Michael C. Rockefeller Memorial
Collection, Bequest of Nelson A.
Rockefeller, 1979   1979.206.24

White-faced masks of this kind were made by Fang sculptors of the Ogowe River in Gabon, Africa. They represent spirit beings and were used ceremonially by both men and women.

1 Start with the bag folded flat, with the bottom of the bag and the seam facing downward. Place the dinner plate face down on the bag, about ¼ inch from the top and side edges. Trace around the plate with the pencil, and set the plate aside. Trim the bag ¼ inch below the circle, reserving the cutoff piece of bag.

2 Open the bag, put it over your head, and mark the position of your eyes with the pencil. Fold the bag flat again and, starting with the eyes, draw the outlines of the mask, using the diagram at right and the picture at above left as your guides. Adjust the position of the eyebrows, nose, and mouth up or down, depending on the position of your eyes.

3 Paint the black border around the mask. When it has dried, thin a little of the white paint with water and brush it over the lower section of the mask lightly, so that some of the paper-bag color can be seen through

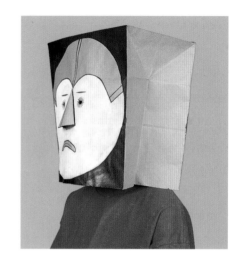

it. When the paint has dried, use the felt-tip pen to darken all the lines and details of the mask, excluding the nose. Make the eye holes by carefully poking through the marked places with the point of the pencil.

4 To make the three-dimensional nose, use the nose template on page 59, and draw the shape on the reserved piece of paper bag. With the felt-tip pen, draw a line down the center of the nose and another along the lower edge.

5 Fold under the outer sections of the nose along the fold lines to make supports for gluing. Put a thin line of glue on the underside of one support. Position it along the corresponding edge of the nose on the mask. Press into place. When the glue has taken hold, repeat on the opposite side of the nose. The nose will bow outward as shown at right.

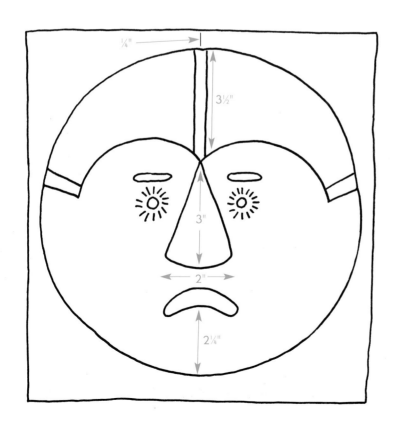

Mrs. Elliott's Wig

ADVANCED

- size 12 paper bag
- pencil
- ruler
- scissors
- 8½" x 11" sheets of paper
- transparent tape
- 1½ yards of ribbon

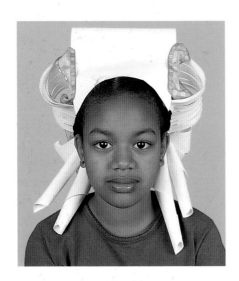

Hairdos were so elaborate in the 18th century that ladies often wore wigs. Hairstyles that were powdered gray or white were the most fashionable.

I Draw the cutting lines on the bag, and cut it as shown in the diagrams at right.

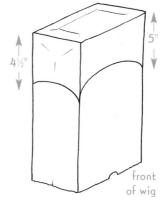

4½"

5"

front of wig

6½"

4½"

back of wig

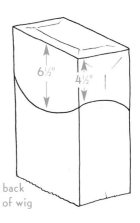

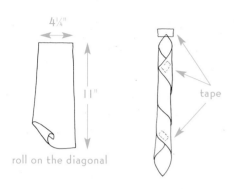

4¼"

11"

roll on the diagonal

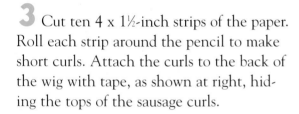

tape

2 Cut eight 4¼ x 11-inch pieces of the paper. Roll each strip on the diagonal to form sausage curls, as shown at left. Secure the curls at the top and bottom by tucking a small roll of tape between the layers. Use tape to attach the curls to the lower back edge of the wig, as shown below.

3 Cut ten 4 x 1½-inch strips of the paper. Roll each strip around the pencil to make short curls. Attach the curls to the back of the wig with tape, as shown at right, hiding the tops of the sausage curls.

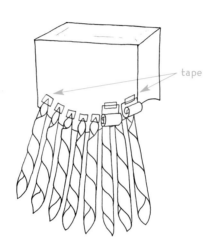

tape

4 Cut another piece of the paper as shown below. Attach the arched end to the front of the wig with small rolls of tape between the layers. Roll the opposite end backward into a fat curl and attach it to the top of the wig with tape, as shown below right.

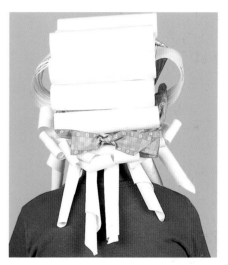

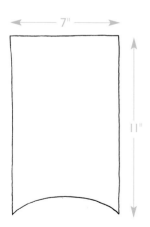

7"

11"

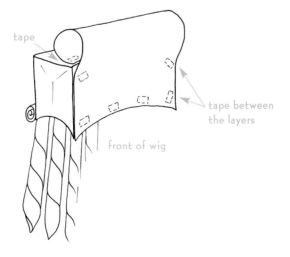

tape

tape between the layers

front of wig

25

Mrs. Elliott's Wig

5 Cut five 7 x 7-inch pieces of the paper. Roll one piece into a fat curl and secure the edge with tape. Tape the curl, seam-side down, across the center top of the wig with small, concealed rolls of tape. Align one end of the next 7 x 7-inch piece of paper across the top back of the wig and tape in place. Roll the opposite end so that it meets the fat curl on top of the wig, and tape it in place. Roll the other three pieces of 7 x 7-inch paper into fat curls and secure them with tape. Arrange them horizontally on the back of the wig, as shown above right, and tape them into place.

6 Cut two more pieces of the paper, as shown at right, folding the paper slightly to start each parallel cut. Leaving a ¼-inch margin at top and bottom, cut the interior of each piece into ¼-inch strips. Attach the pieces to the sides of the wig with tape along the top and bottom edges so that the side pieces bulge outward.

7 Wrap the ribbon around the wig, threading it through the hair on the sides, and tying it into a bow at the back.

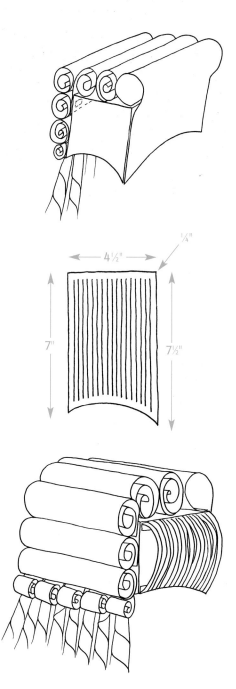

Headddress
Egypt, Dynasty 18, ca. 1482–1450 B.C.
Gold, carnelian, turquoise glass, and clear glass, max. Diam. 12 in.
Purchase, Frederick P. Huntley Bequest, 1958   58.153.2,3;
Purchase, Lila Acheson Wallace Gift, 1982, 1983   1982.137,
1983.1–13; Purchase, Joseph Pulitzer Bequest, 1966   66.2.77;
Fletcher Fund, 1926   26.8.117a

Egyptian Queen's Headdress

EASY

In ancient Egypt, royal women often enhanced their hairstyles with gold jewelry. This headdress, worn by one of the queens of King Tuthmosis III, is inlaid with thousands of tiny pieces of colored glass and stone.

size 12 or 16 paper bag
pencil
ruler
scissors
glitter glue

1 Start with the bag folded flat. Cut the bag crosswise 9 inches from the bottom. Then cut the bag along one side so that it measures 5 inches wide. Discard the cutoff pieces.

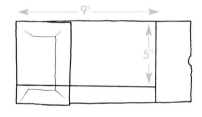

2 Open the bag out. Cut along the two remaining long corner folds and lay the bag flat.

3 Using the ruler, measure and draw lines 1 inch apart on each section of the bag.

4 Use the glitter glue to decorate between the ruled lines.

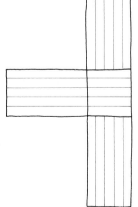

5 Cut along the ruled lines on the side and back panels of the bag.

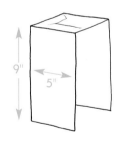

27

Perseus' Winged Helmet

INTERMEDIATE

size 12 or 16 paper bag

pencil

ruler

scissors

white glue or transparent tape

construction paper or other mediumweight craft paper

When the mythological Greek hero Perseus wore his winged helmet, it made him invisible. Wearing the helmet allowed Perseus to sneak up on the monster Medusa and slay her.

Perseus with the Head of Medusa (detail)
Antonio Canova, Italian, 1757–1822
Marble, H. 86⅛ in., 1804–06
Fletcher Fund, 1967   67.110.1

1 Draw the cutting lines on the bag and cut it as shown in the illustrations below.

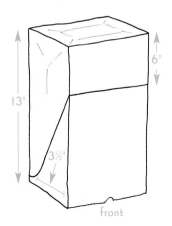

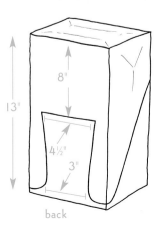

2 Place the bag, folded flat, on a work surface so that the bottom section faces upward. Fold in the four corners of the bottom of the bag evenly, as shown at right.

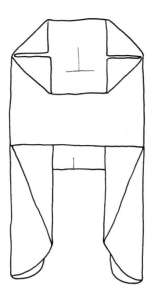

3 Fold the bottom of the bag in half along the center fold line, matching the edges along all three sides. Glue or tape the edges together, as shown below.

4 When the glue has dried, open the helmet out. Tilt the peak of the helmet so that it slants forward slightly.

5 Using the template on page 60, draw the outline of the wing twice on construction paper and cut out the two wings.

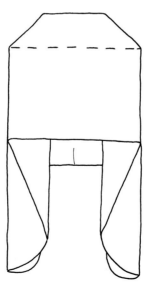

6 Glue or tape the wings to the sides of the helmet, lining up the end of each wing with the edge of the helmet.

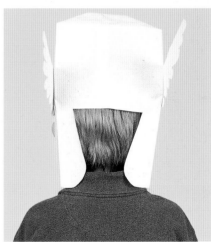

29

Queen of Sheba's Crown

EASY

small gold gift bag
[7" x 8¾" x 3¾"]

scissors

pencil

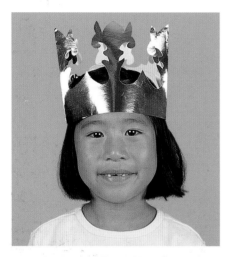

The biblical queen of Sheba, depicted in this tapestry, wears a dress and crown like those of a European queen of about 1500.

Two Riddles of the Queen of Sheba (detail)
Upper Rhenish (Strasbourg), 1490–1500
Bast fiber warp, wool, silk, and metallic wefts, wool pile yarns,
31½ x 40 in.
The Cloisters Collection, 1971   1971.43

1 Cut out the bottom of the bag and fold the bag flat. Trace and cut out the crown template on page 61. Place it on the bag so that the side and bottom edges of the template and bag line up, as shown at right.

2 Draw the outline of the crown on the bag and cut it out, cutting through both layers of the bag.

(If your bag is a slightly different size than the template, center the template on the bag and draw the outline of the center point of the crown. Then line up the left side of the template with the left side of the bag and trace the outline of the left point of the crown. Repeat on the right side. Then draw the lines that connect the three points freehand.)

Pharaoh's Headdress

ADVANCED

Hatshepsut was one of the few female pharaohs of ancient Egypt. She was often depicted wearing the nemes *headcloth, a traditional headdress of pharaohs, as well as a ceremonial false beard.*

Kneeling Figure of Queen Hatshepsut (detail)
Thebes, Deir el Bahri, Temple of Hatshepsut,
Dynasty 18, ca. 1503–1482 B.C.
Red granite, H. 8 ft. 7 in.
Rogers Fund, 1929   29.3.1
Photograph by Schecter Lee

small grocery bag
[10¼" x 14¼" x 6⅛"]

pencil

ruler

scissors

white glue

acrylic paint [blue, gold]

paintbrush

black felt-tip pen

1 Start with the bag folded flat and the bottom and seam of the bag facing downward. Cut the bag crosswise 10 inches from the bottom. Discard the cutoff piece.

2 Cut away the front panel of the bag, leaving a 3-inch margin, as shown at right. Reserve the cutoff piece of bag. Open the bag and turn it bottom-side up.

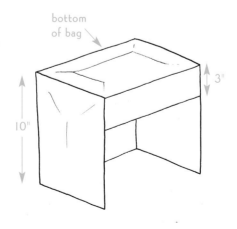

bottom
of bag

3"

10"

Pharaoh's Headdress

3 Carefully cut the bag as shown in bold in the diagrams below.

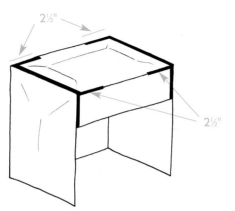

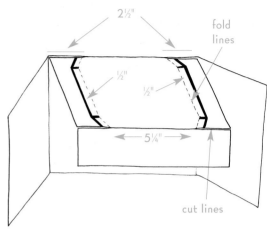

4 Fold down the ½-inch edges along each side of the top, making a sharp crease, as shown below left. Then wrap the ends of the front band to the back on each side and glue in place, as shown below right.

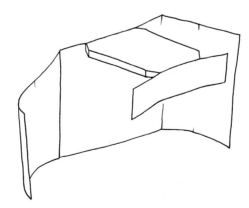

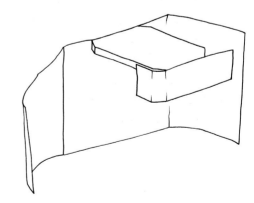

5 Bring the side back sections of the bag forward, as shown at right, using the natural creases in the bag to create the back flaps of the headdress.

6 Glue the side sections in place. Cut the tops of the back flaps on the diagonal and glue the cuts closed.

7 Paint stripes on the headdress, if desired.

8 To make the cobra, use the template on page 60, cutting the shape from the reserved piece of bag.

9 Paint the cobra gold. When the paint has dried, use the felt-tip pen to color the eyes and to decorate the cobra's belly. Fold it as shown in the diagram at right. Glue the cobra in place on the front of the headdress.

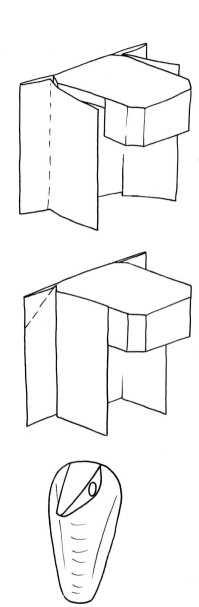

Greek Goddess Hairstyle

INTERMEDIATE

size 12 paper bag

pencil

ruler

scissors

7" x 10½" piece of paper

white glue or transparent tape

two 30" pieces of ½"-wide ribbon, or ½"-wide strips of colored paper glued together to make two 30" strips

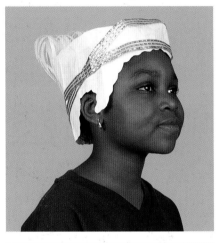

Kylix
Attributed to the Villa Giulia Painter
Greek, Attic, ca. 470 B.C. Terracotta,
W. (including handles) 8¼ in.
The Bothmer Purchase Fund, Fletcher Fund,
and Rogers Fund, 1979   1979.11.15

This goddess is wearing her hair in a style often shown in ancient Greek art, pulled up and bound with ribbons.

I Draw the cutting lines on the bag and cut it as shown in the diagrams below, making a wavy edge as you cut. Discard the cutoff pieces.

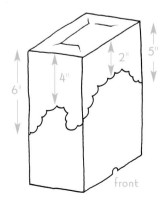

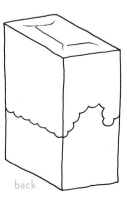

2 Tuck in the corners and edges on the top of the wig, as shown in the Basic Instructions, page 11.

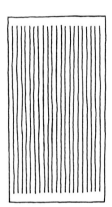

3 Cut the 7 x 10½-inch piece of paper into ¼-inch strips, leaving a ½-inch margin at top and bottom, as shown at left. Fold the paper slightly to start each parallel cut.

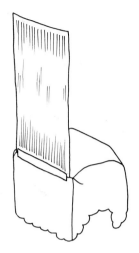

4 Glue or tape one end of the stripped paper to the top back of the wig, as shown above right.

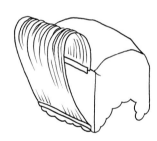

5 Roll the stripped paper downward and glue or tape the loose end in place at the bottom back of the wig, as shown at right.

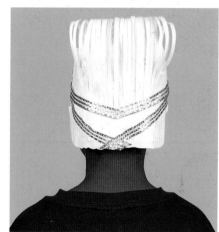

6 Using the photographs at right and the diagram below right as guides for placement, wrap one of the ribbons around the wig, gluing or taping it in place at intervals. Repeat with the second ribbon.

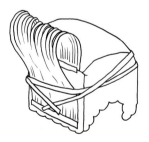

Napoléon's Crown

EASY

small gold gift bag [7" x 8¾" x 3¾"]

pencil

ruler

scissors

transparent tape

When Napoléon Bonaparte crowned himself emperor in Paris in 1804, he wore a crown of gold leaves like the emperors of ancient Rome.

Portrait of Napoléon I (detail)
French, Gobelins Manufactory
Designed by François Gérard (1770–1837) in 1805
Tapestry woven of wool, silk, and silver-gilt thread,
87½ x 57½ in., 1808–11
Purchase, Joseph Pulitzer Bequest, 1943   43.99
Photograph by Schecter Lee

1 Draw the outline of the crown on the bag as shown in the diagrams at right. Draw pointed leaf shapes along the top edge of the crown, and scallop the bottom edge. Cut out the crown.

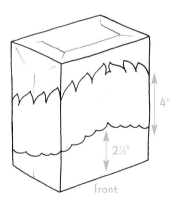

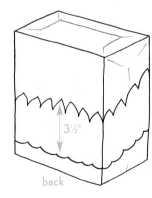

front

back

4"

2½"

3½"

2 Using the remaining part of the bag and the templates on page 62, cut out twelve large and twelve small golden leaves.

3 Decorate the front of the bag with the golden leaves. Place a small roll of tape on the back of each leaf. Working from center front outward, arrange the leaves on the diagonal, facing the center, overlapping the edges.

Stylish Hat with Stand-Up Fringe

INTERMEDIATE

In the first two decades of the 20th century, women's fashions lost their Victorian fussiness and became entirely modern, as shown by this amazing hat from about 1914.

Hat
American, ca. 1914
Black silk velvet with feathers and beaded hatpin
Label: F. P. O'Connor Co., Boston
Gift of Art Worker's Club, 1945   CI 45.68.47

size 16 paper bag

pencil

ruler

scissors

white glue

transparent tape

11" x 14" sheet of construction paper

glitter glue

1 Start with the bag folded flat. Cut the bag crosswise 3¾ inches from the bottom. Open the bag and set it bottom-side up to form the crown of the hat. Reserve the cutoff piece.

2 Take the reserved piece of bag, open out the side folds, and lay it flat. Mark and then cut the bag to make two pieces, as shown at right.

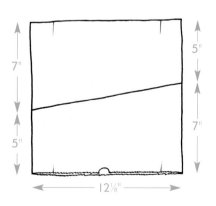

7"
5"
5"
7"
12⅛"

Stylish Hat with Stand-Up Fringe

3 Open out the two pieces and pull one over the other so that their heights correspond as shown below left. Then pull the two pieces over the crown of the hat, as shown below right, so that the bottom edges of all three layers meet evenly all the way around. Glue or insert pieces of rolled tape between the layers on each side.

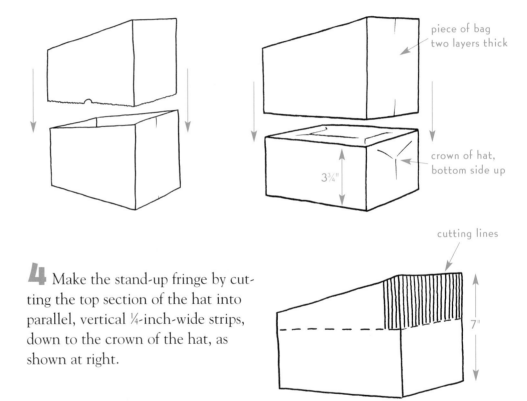

piece of bag two layers thick

crown of hat, bottom side up

3¾"

cutting lines

4 Make the stand-up fringe by cutting the top section of the hat into parallel, vertical ¼-inch-wide strips, down to the crown of the hat, as shown at right.

7"

5 To make the hatband, cut the piece of construction paper lengthwise down the middle. Glue or tape the two pieces together to make one strip about 27 inches long.

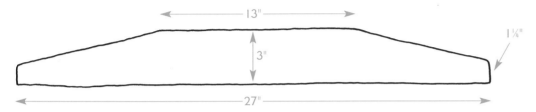

6 Cut the strip so that it is 3 inches high in the center and 1¼ inches high at either end, as shown above.

7 Wrap the band around the hat so that the height of the band corresponds with the height of the fringe. Glue or tape the hatband in place.

8 Cut a 1½-inch-wide circle out of a scrap of construction paper or paper bag. Decorate it with the glitter glue. When dry, attach it to the hat with glue or tape.

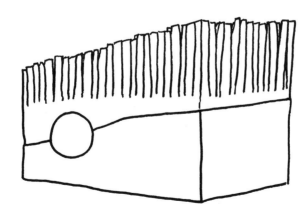

Mrs. Mayer's Bonnet

ADVANCED

size 12 paper bag

pencil

ruler

scissors

two 8½" x 11" sheets of lightweight paper

white glue

hole punch

paper clips

1 yard of ribbon cut in half

Ammi Phillips was one of the most talented American folk artists of the 19th century. His images are strong because he focused on his subjects' faces and costumes against dark backgrounds.

1 Start with the bag lying flat and the bottom of the bag facing upward. Cut the bag as shown at right.

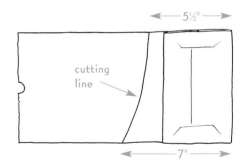

5½"

cutting line

7"

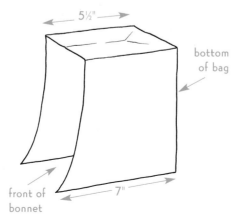

5½"

bottom of bag

front of bonnet

7"

2 Open the bag and cut out the narrow side of the bag that measures seven inches long, as shown at left. The bottom of the bag will form the back of the bonnet.

3 Fold the two sheets of 8½ x 11-inch paper lengthwise into thirds. Then cut the sheets along the fold lines into strips.

4 Glue two of the strips together end to end, overlapping the ends slightly, to make one long strip. Separately, glue the other four strips together to make one extra-long strip.

5 Cut one long edge of each strip into 1½-inch-wide scallops, as shown at right. Then punch holes along the scalloped edge to create "lace."

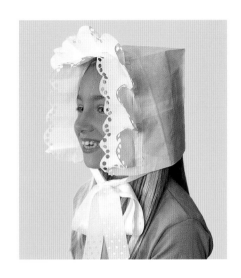

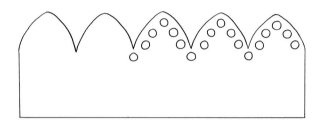

6 Take the shorter of the two strips and fold it into ½-inch accordion folds, as shown at left. Open the strip out again until it retains just a slightly ruffled surface.

7 Put a thin line of glue along the outside of one side of the bonnet opening. Starting at a lower front corner, glue the ruffled strip, scalloped side facing out, along the edge of the bonnet. Continue gluing the ruffled strip along the top and the other side edge.

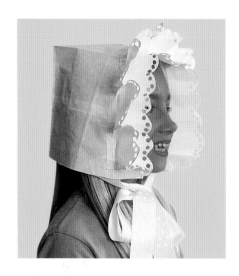

8 Take the extra long strip. Working along the straight edge of the strip, make one ½-inch accordion tuck about every three inches. Leave the scalloped edge of the strip loose and ruffled.

9 Glue the tucks closed, using a small dot of glue on the inside folds of each tuck. Secure the tucks with paper clips while they dry, as shown at right.

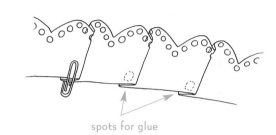

spots for glue

10 When the glue has dried, remove the paper clips. Make a ½-inch-deep fold all the way along the straight edge of the strip, as shown at right. This will make the ruffled edge stand up.

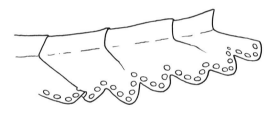

11 Using the ½-inch-deep fold as the gluing surface, glue the ruffle in place around the front of the bonnet, covering the edge of the previously glued strip. Allow the glue to dry.

12 Cut the ribbon in half. Glue the two pieces to the inside front corners of the bonnet. Allow the glue to dry.

1920s Cloche
ADVANCED

size 16 paper bag
ruler
transparent tape
pencil
scissors
white glue

Cloche
American, russet silk velvet
and feathers, ca. 1924
Gift of Julia B. Henry, 1978
1978.288.4b

One of the most popular hat styles of the 1920s was the cloche, which is the French word for "bell." The cloche had a shallow brim or no brim at all, and was pulled down low over the forehead to accentuate the eyes.

1 Open the bag. Make a cuff by folding the open end of the bag to the inside, to a depth of about 3½ inches, as shown at right. Crease the fold.

3½"

2 Then pull the open end back out so that it extends 1 inch beyond the fold, forming a cuff. Secure the cuff by taping the inside of the fold with tape, as shown at left.

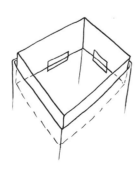

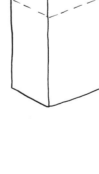

43

1920s Cloche

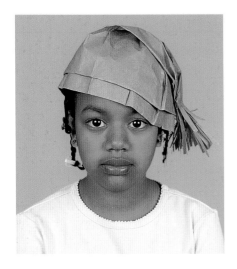

3 Cut away the bottom of the bag. Then cut away the top section of one of the wide sides of the bag, leaving a 5-inch border above the cuff, as shown at right. Reserve the cutoff pieces of bag.

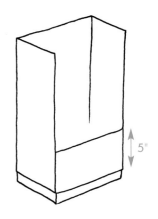

4 Place the bag on your head, as shown at left, with the cut section of the bag to one side. Pull the cuff of the bag over your forehead, angled downward toward the cut side of the bag.

5 Using both hands, fold the top of the bag down toward the cut side, gathering and tucking the paper into folds as you go, shaping it to fit your head snugly.

6 Holding the end of the bag in place, remove the hat from your head. Shape the end of the folded section into a "V." Tape or glue the V in place.

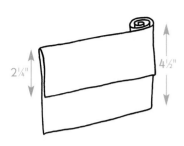

2¼" 4½"

7 To make the feathery trim for the hat, use the reserved piece cut from the side of the bag. Hold the piece horizontally and fold over the top 2¼ inches to make a cuff. Then roll it up with the cuff facing outward, as shown at left. When rolled, secure the top with tape.

8 Insert one scissor point in the bottom of the roll and cut the roll into ⅛-inch strips, stopping when you reach the tape at the top.

9 Cut a 3 x ¾-inch strip from the reserved bottom of the bag. Wrap it around the top of the feathery trim to hide the tape. Glue the end in place.

10 When completed, fluff the strips lightly to give them a feathery look. Glue the trim in place on the side of the hat, where the folded V meets the cuff.

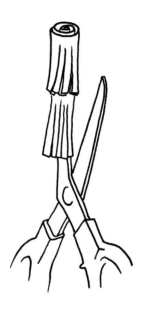

45

George Washington's Hair

EASY

size 12 paper bag

pencil

ruler

scissors

white glue or transparent tape

30" piece of ribbon or string

Like many gentlemen of the 18th century, George Washington powdered his hair to make it white, and tied it behind in a ponytail, or queue.

George Washington (detail)
Gilbert Stuart, American, 1755–1828
Oil on canvas, 30¼ x 25¼ in.
Rogers Fund, 1907   07.160

1 Draw the cutting lines on the bag and cut it as shown in the drawings below. Reserve the cutoff pieces.

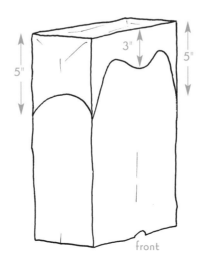

front

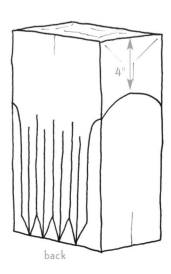

back

2 Cut the back section into strips to make "hair," trimming the ends with zigzag cuts.

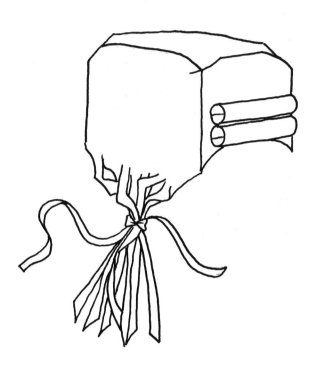

3 To give the wig a rounder shape on top, tuck in the corners, as shown in the Basic Instructions, page 11.

4 Using parts of the bag that have been cut away, cut four 4-inch-wide strips at least 3 inches long.

5 Roll the strips, securing the ends with glue or tape. Glue or tape the rolls in place on the sides of the wig.

6 Tie the hair in back with a piece of ribbon or string, tying a bow.

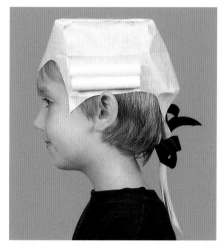

Curly Baroque Wig

ADVANCED

- size 16 paper bag
- pencil
- ruler
- scissors
- 3 large grocery bags
- white glue
- transparent tape

Most European gentlemen wore wigs with their dress clothes in the 17th and 18th centuries, and generals wore elaborately curled wigs even with their armor.

[Portrait of] Alexander Menshikov (1673–1729)
Swiss, Austrian, or German sculptor, active in
Russia ca. 1703–04
Red pine, H. (with socle) 30⅝ in.
Wrightsman Fund, 1996   1996.7

1 Start with the bag lying flat. Cut it crosswise 8 inches from the bottom.

2 Open the bag and stand it bottom-side up. Draw and then cut an arch, 4 inches wide and 6½ inches tall, out of one of the narrow sides of the bag, as shown at right. Pull the bag over your head to make sure the arch does not block your eyes. Adjust the width of the arch if necessary.

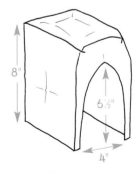

3 Tuck in the front corners of the bag, as shown in the Basic Instructions, page 11.

4 Cut the bottom out of one of the grocery bags and discard. Cut the remaining portion of the bag into 1 x 3-inch strips.

5 Placing one of the narrow sides of a strip against a pencil, tightly wrap the strip to make a curl. (The tighter you wrap the strip, the better.)

6 Starting at the top of the wig, working from the center outward, put a little white glue on the end of the curl, and glue it in place. Cutting additional strips from the other two bags as necessary, continue to make and glue curls onto the top, sides, back, and front of the wig, stopping about 2 inches from the bottom.

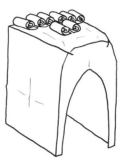

7 Cut sixteen 1½ x 15-inch strips out of the remaining paper bag. Roll each strip on the diagonal to make a 4-inch to 6-inch sausage curl, as shown at left. Secure each sausage curl with rolls of tape or small dabs of glue between the folds so that it holds its shape.

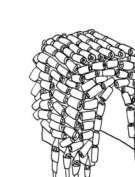

8 Glue or tape the sausage curls around the bottom of the bag so that they dangle loosely, as shown at right. Try the wig on to make sure that the curls are not too long. Trim the curls if necessary.

9 Continue to make and glue more 1 x 3-inch curls in place to cover the tops of the sausage curls. Glue additional small curls along the lengths of the sausage curls.

10 If it appears that some of the curls are going to lose their shape after they dry, secure them with a little glue.

Dutch Woman's Cap

EASY

size 16 paper bag

scissors

ruler

pencil

Young Woman with a Water Jug
Johannes Vermeer, Dutch, 1632–1675
Oil on canvas, 18 x 16 in.
Marquand Collection, Gift of Henry G.
Marquand, 1889   89.15.21

In the 1600s, when Johannes Vermeer painted this interior scene in the Netherlands, middle-class women kept their hair covered most of the time, even when they were indoors.

1 Open the bag. Cut away one of the narrow sides of the bag, then turn back the edge to make a 1-inch cuff.

2 Tuck in the back top corners, as shown in the Basic Instructions, page 11.

3 Cut the lower edge of the cap on the diagonal, as in the diagram at right.

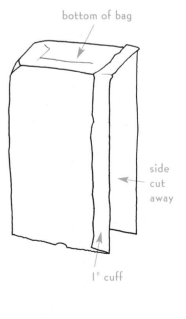

bottom of bag

side cut away

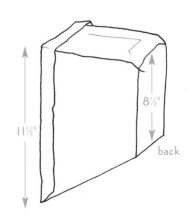

11½"

8½"

back

1" cuff

50

Funerary Mask
Peru (Sicán), 9th–11th century
Gold, paint; H. 11½ in.
Gift and Bequest of Alice K. Bache,
1974, 1977   1974.271.35
Photograph by Schecter Lee

Sicán Mask

INTERMEDIATE

large grocery bag
[12" x 17" x 6⅞"]

pencil

ruler

scissors

acrylic paint [red, black,
white, blue, green, gold]

paintbrush

black felt-tip pen

white glue

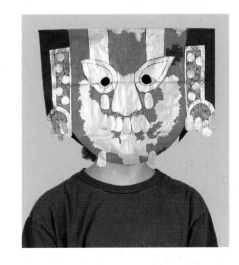

Wealthy and powerful lords of the Sicán dynasty in Peru were buried with their golden treasures, including masks. As many as five masks might be placed in one burial.

1 Start with the bag folded flat, and the bottom of the bag and the seam facing downward. Draw the outlines of the mask on the bag using the diagram at right as a guide.

2 Cut out the mask along the lower edge only, cutting through the front and back layers of the bag. Reserve the cutoff piece. Open the bag, place it over your head, center it, and mark the position of your eyes.

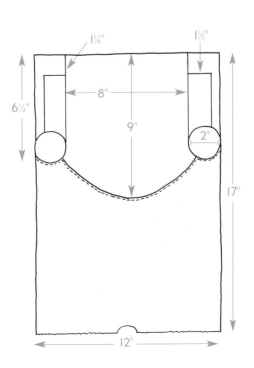

Sicán Mask

3 Fold the bag flat again, and draw the details of the face as shown in the diagram below.

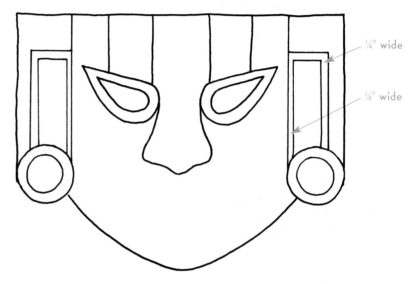

¼" wide

⅛" wide

4 Paint the bag as shown in the photographs at left. Allow each color to dry before adding the next one. Stipple the edges of the gold areas by putting just a small amount of the paint on the tip of the brush and then dabbing the brush up and down on the bag. To create the blue-green areas, first paint them solid green. Then stipple the areas with a little of the black paint. Finally, stipple the areas again with a pastel mixture of the blue, green, and white paint.

5 When the paint is dry, use the felt-tip pen to outline the features and create the details on the mask. Cut out the eye holes.

6 Using the reserved piece of bag, paint a 6-inch-square section gold. When the paint is dry, draw ten ½-inch circles and twenty 1-inch drops, like those at right, on the gold square.

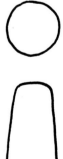

7 Cut out the circles and drops. Put a small dab of glue at the top of each, and position them on the mask, as shown in the photographs above left.

Courtesan Holding a Fan
Kitagawa Utamaro, Japanese, 1753?–1806
Woodcut, 14½ x 9⅝ in., ca. 1793
Rogers Fund, 1922   JP 1367

Japanese Beauty's Wig
ADVANCED

In Japanese tradition, elaborate hairstyles were part of the ideal of feminine beauty. A woman's hair was treated with wax to help the hairstyle hold its shape, and a special pillow was required for sleeping.

size 12 paper bag

pencil

ruler

scissors

2 small grocery bags
[10¼" x 14¼" x 6⅛"]

white glue

coffee can or oatmeal box

small piece of colored paper
[at least 7" x 3"]

8½" x 11" sheet of white paper

light-blue colored pencil

1 Draw the cutting lines on the size 12 bag. Cut the bag as shown below. Discard the cutoff piece.

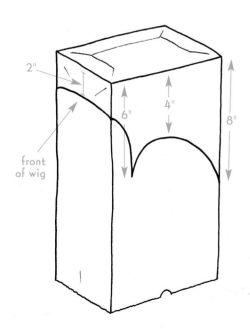

2"

6"

4"

8"

front of wig

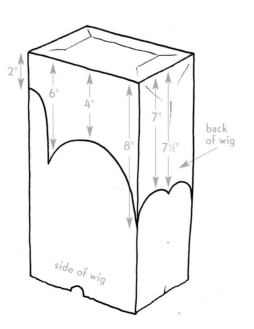

2"

6"

4"

8"

7"

7½"

back of wig

side of wig

Japanese Beauty's Wig

2 Tuck in the four corners of the bag as shown in the Basic Instructions, page 11. This will be the wig base.

3 Select one of the small grocery bags. Cut it along the seam and then cut out the bottom of the bag. Spread the bag flat. Centered on one long edge of the flattened bag, draw and then cut out an arch, as shown below.

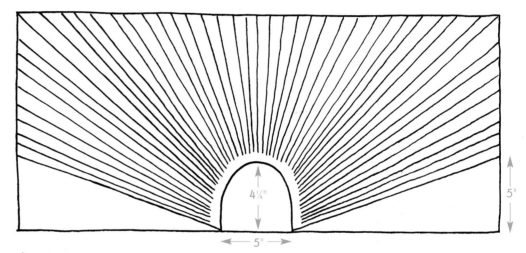

4¼"

5"

5"

4 Starting at the top center of the arch, draw lines that radiate from the arch as shown above. The lines should begin about ½ inch away from the arch and should be about ¼ inch wide at the narrow end and between ¾ and 1¼ inch wide at the outer edge. (Don't worry about being too exact, because the wide ends of the strips will not be visible on the completed wig.) Cut along the radiating lines, stopping ½ inch away from the arch. This will be the "hair."

5 Turn the wig base upside down, with the front facing toward you. Put a thin line of glue along the front edge of the wig base. Then pick up the hair from step 4 so that the arch is upside down. Starting on the left, carefully glue the edge of the arch around the front edge of the wig base, as shown at right. Allow the glue to dry.

6 Use the coffee can, oatmeal box, or similar object as a wig stand. Turn the wig base right side up and place it on the stand. Let the hair fall forward, toward you.

7 Starting at center front, lift one strand of hair and bend it back toward the top of the wig base, making a slight pouf at the front. Attach the strand to the top of the wig base with a dot of glue about 2 inches from the front. Repeat with the other strands that cover the top of the wig (about 14 to 16 strands in all). Glue the ends of the strands of hair in place on the back of the wig.

8 Starting at the top of each side, lift each strand of hair and roll it backward to make a fat loop. Trim the end and glue it to the wig base. Graduate the length of the loops so that they are longer toward the bottom of each side. If there is not room enough to make loops from the lowest strands of hair on each side, simply pull them back, trim them, and glue them in place inside the lowest loop.

9 Cut along the seam of the remaining small grocery bag, and then cut out the bottom of the bag. Spread the bag flat. Cut an 8 x 14¼-inch piece from the bag, reserving the rest of the bag. Leaving a ½-inch border at either end, cut the piece into ¼-inch strips. Fold the paper slightly to start each parallel cut.

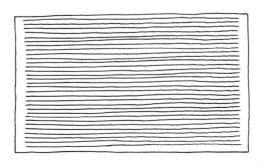

10 Put a thin line of glue along one border of the piece. Turn the border under, and glue it in place just behind the pouf at the front of the wig, as shown below. At the opposite end of the piece, cut the border at the center point. Lap one half over the other, as shown below, and glue into place.

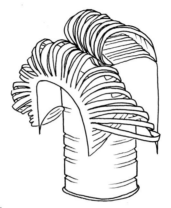
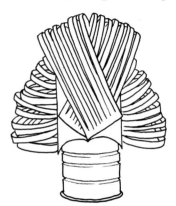

11 Cut two 3 x 14¼-inch pieces from the reserved piece of the bag. Leaving a ½-inch border at either end, cut each piece into ¼-inch strips, as in step 9. Use these pieces to fill in the sides of the wig, rolling one end under and gluing it just behind the side poufs of hair, crossing the two pieces and gluing them in the back, as shown below.

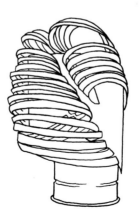
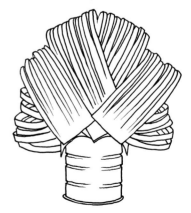

12 If there are any empty spaces remaining on the wig, repeat step 11, with extra pieces of paper to fill in.

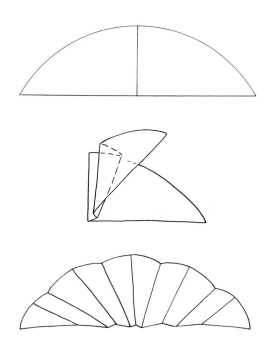

13 To make the colorful "comb" hair ornament, use the comb template on page 63. Draw the outline of the shape on a piece of the colored paper and cut it out. Fold the comb in half, matching the outer points. Working from the center outward, make diagonal folds that are wide at the top and narrow at the bottom. Then open and flatten the comb and glue it in place just behind the front pouf of the wig.

14 To make the white hair ornaments, cut two pieces of the white paper, 2½ x 11 inches. Roll each piece tightly on the diagonal to form a long tube that is slightly wider at one end than the other, as shown at right. (It's easiest if you roll the paper over a pencil.) Glue the end in place. Cut out two flower shapes like the one below, and decorate them with the colored pencil. Glue one flower on the wide end of each hair ornament. Arrange the ornaments in the wig, sticking them through the pouf at the front of the hairdo.

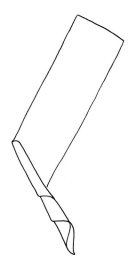

Templates

Use the templates on the following pages as needed. Begin by copying a template onto tracing paper and cutting it out. Then, trace the template's outline onto construction paper or other craft paper and cut out the shape. If the template has any decorations, don't forget to add them to the shape.

fold line

Side piece and front band for the God of Wealth's Hat

Top crest for
the God of
Wealth's Hat

Nose for the
Fang Mask

fold line

fold line

Flowers, leaf,
and stem for the
Flower-Decorated
Cloche

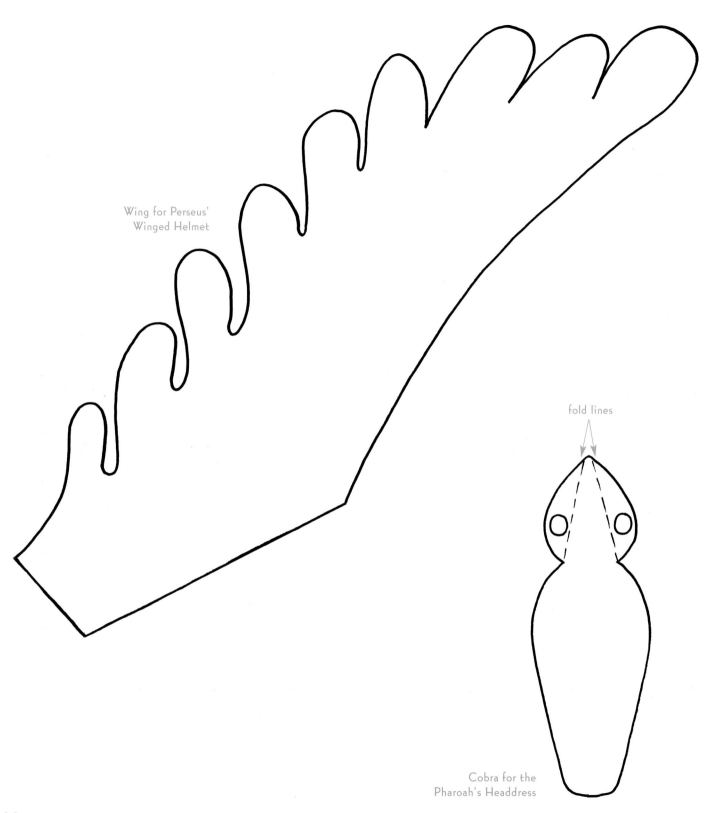

Wing for Perseus'
Winged Helmet

fold lines

Cobra for the
Pharoah's Headdress

The Queen of Sheba's Crown

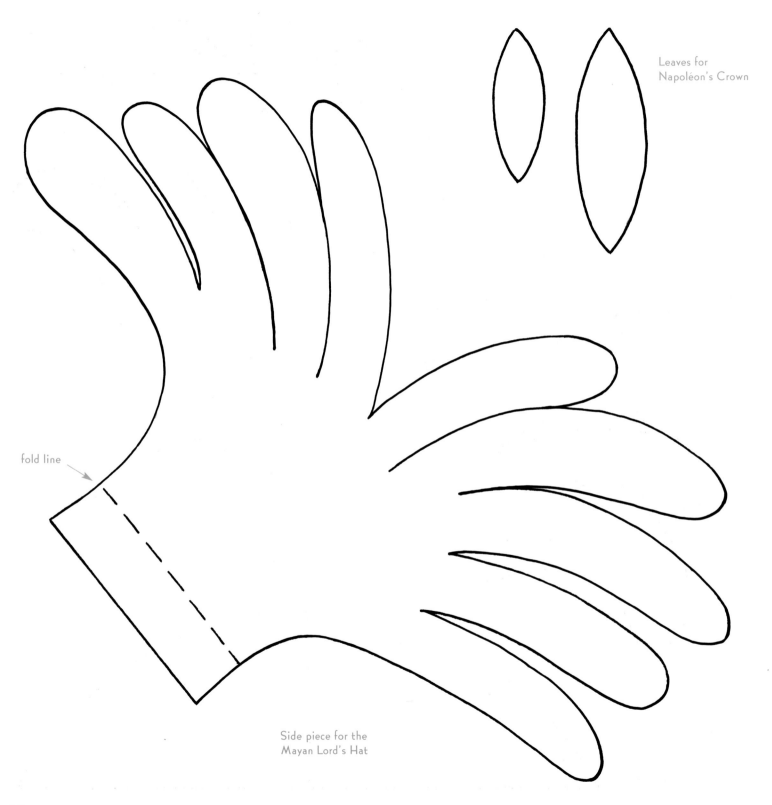

Leaves for
Napoléon's Crown

fold line

Side piece for the
Mayan Lord's Hat